The Indians Knew

_____ _IE S. PINE_

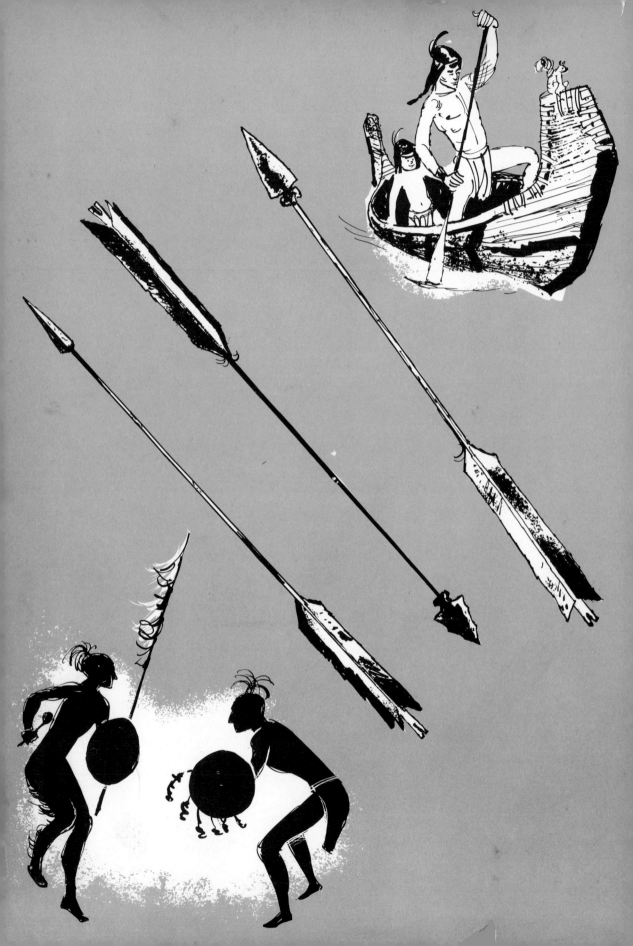

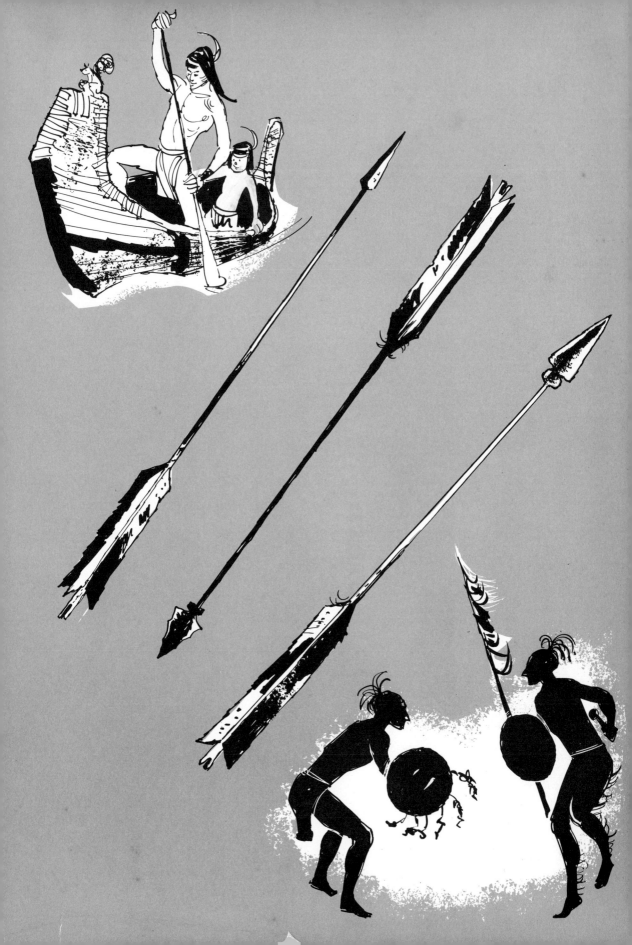

The Indians Knew

THE Indians

WHITTLESEY HOUSE

McGRAW-HILL BOOK COMPANY, INC.

New York   Toronto   London

Knew

BY TILLIE S. PINE

PICTURES BY EZRA JACK KEATS

This book is dedicated to
Stanley Weiss and Joseph Levine
for their invaluable assistance

Library of Congress Catalog Card Number:
57–6405

Published by Whittlesey House,
a division of the McGraw-Hill Book Company, Inc.

Printed in the United States of America

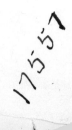

Do you know that the Indians who lived in our country long, long ago knew how to do many things that we do today?

They knew

How to send messages across mountains

How to make plants grow better

How to prevent food from spoiling

How to start a fire without matches

How to drill holes

How to make paints and dyes

How to use the moon as a calendar.

In this book you will read about some of the many, many things that the Indians knew. You will do some science activities that will help you understand why the Indians did the things they did to help them in their day-to-day living.

The Indians knew how!

You will know why!

Kithy

The Indians knew

that wood could be bent to make
things spring rapidly through the air.
They bent pieces of wood into bows.
They used these to shoot off arrows.

Today

divers jump off the end of a springboard.
The weight of the diver bends the springboard.
As he jumps, the board straightens. This
pushes the diver up into the air and makes
it easier for him to dive.

You

can prove that wood can be bent to make
things move fast.
Hold one end of a wooden ruler on the table
so that most of the ruler extends over the
edge. Place an eraser on the free end of
the ruler. Bend this end down and quickly
let it go. The eraser will fly into the air
as soon as you let go of the free end of the
ruler.

The Indians knew

that smoke rises.

When Indians built a tepee they always left
an opening at the top.   In this way, when
they sat around the fire in the tepee and
listened to the wise man tell stories, they
were sure the smoke from the fire would rise
and escape through the opening.

The Indians also sent smoke messages to their
friends.

They built a campfire.   The smoke from the
campfire rose high into the air.   Then they
made smoke puffs by covering and uncovering
the fire quickly with a blanket or an animal
skin.   When their friends saw the smoke puffs
they "read" the message and understood.

Today

we build tall chimneys in fireplaces to let
the smoke go up and out toward the sky.
We also open windows at the top to let
warm air out to cool off the room.

You

can prove that warm air and smoke rise.
Blow up a balloon and hold it over a warm
radiator. Watch the balloon rise when
the air warmed by the radiator makes it
go up.
Hold a strip of tissue paper in your hand.
Watch how the paper is lifted up when you
hold it over a warm radiator.
Watch when someone blows out a match.
See how the smoke rises.

The Indians knew

how to shape bark or animal skin so that it could carry them on the water. They shaped bark and animal skin into canoes. These canoes were light and hollow. They could easily be paddled down the river, up the river, or out into the sea.

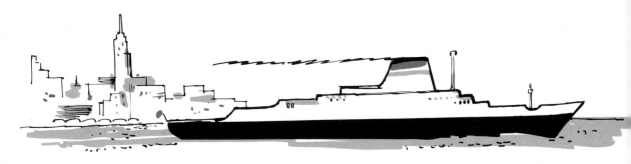

Today

we make small rowboats and large ships by
shaping them so that they can travel on water
to near and far places. Large ships have many
hollow spaces inside to keep them afloat.

You

can prove how the shape of things helps to
carry things on water.
Put a piece of paper on some water in a basin.
Place a few coins on the paper. You will see
that the paper sinks as soon as the coins fall on it.
Now fold another piece of paper into the shape of a
box. Place the paper box with some coins in it on
the water in the basin. The box-shaped paper will
carry the coins on the water and will not sink as
long as the paper does not soak through.

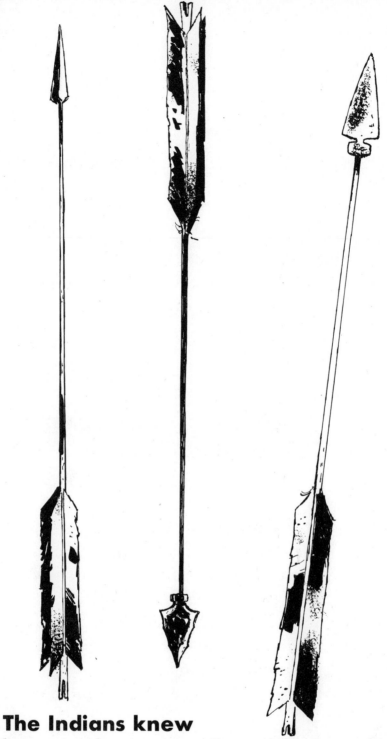

The Indians knew

how to make an arrow fly straight through
the air.
They put feathers at the end of the arrow to
keep it flying in a straight line.

Today

we build "tail fins" on airplanes to help the planes fly in a straight line.

You

can find out how to throw a drinking straw so that it will fly through the air in a straight line.

First you throw the straw across the room. You will see that the straw will fall to the ground immediately. Then you cut two cross slits in one end of the straw. Put two strips of paper into the slits. Now throw the straw across the room. Do you see that the straw with the tail fins flies through the air in a straight line?

The Indians knew

that they could make work easier by pulling
things instead of carrying them.
They took two long, strong branches and made
a "drag." This was also called a "travois"
(tra-vwah'). Some Indians moved often from
place to place. These Indians used the travois
to drag the household things they took with
them when they moved.

Today

when mother takes home the food she buys in
the food market, she makes it easier for herself
by pulling her purchases home in a cart.
And to make the job easier still, we have put
the drag on wheels.

You

can prove that pulling is easier than carrying
by doing this:
Carry a heavy bundle of books, a small radio,
or a heavy basket across the room.
Now put each of these heavy things on a chair.
Tilt the chair and pull it across the room.

Do you agree that pulling is easier than carrying?

The Indians knew

how to keep some foods from spoiling by
drying them.   They dried meat and fish
by hanging these foods in the sunshine.
They also dried these foods over their
fires.   Now the meat and fish could keep for a
long time without spoiling.

Today

we dry some fruits and vegetables in order to keep them from spoiling. We dry grapes in the hot sun to get raisins. We dry plums to get prunes.

You

can prove that when foods have been dried they do not spoil even if they are not kept in a cool place.

Place a few grapes and plums and a few raisins and prunes in a dish. Leave them uncovered on the table for a few days.

At the end of that time, examine the food in the dish. Do you see that the raisins and the prunes have not spoiled because they had been dried before Mother bought them?

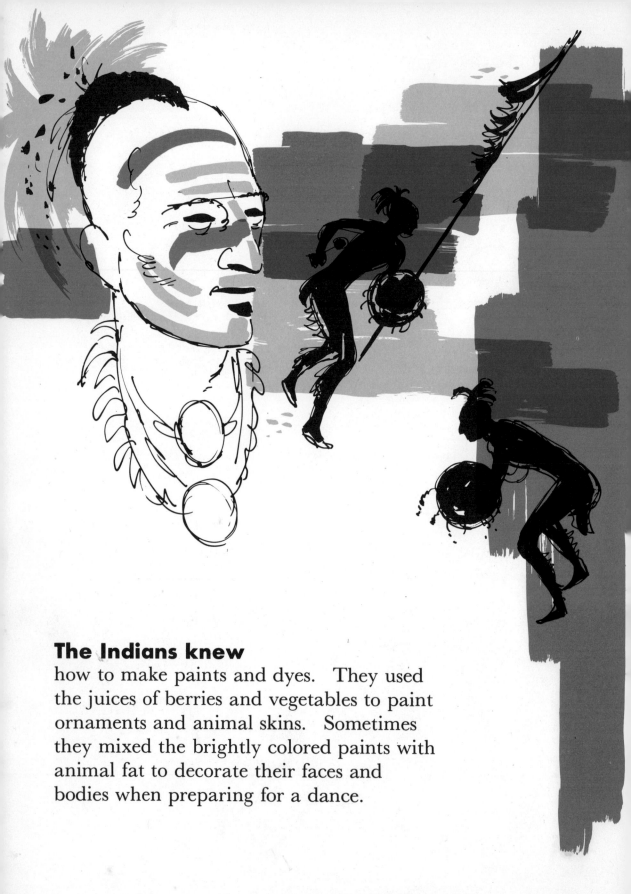

The Indians knew

how to make paints and dyes. They used
the juices of berries and vegetables to paint
ornaments and animal skins. Sometimes
they mixed the brightly colored paints with
animal fat to decorate their faces and
bodies when preparing for a dance.

Today

we use vegetable coloring to paint the
toys that are used by children.

You

can make your own dyes very simply.
Squeeze some raspberries or blackberries
or strawberries into a dish.
Place a sliced beet in a little water in
another dish.
Dip a small piece of white cloth into the
juice of the berries.
Now dip another piece of white cloth into
the juice of the beet.
You will notice that the cloths have two
colors dyed right into them – the color of
the berries and the color of the beet.

The Indians knew

that sound goes through the ground.
When they wanted to hear sounds from
far off they put their ears to the ground
and listened.

Today

we knock on the door before we enter a room.
The sound goes through the solid door. It then
travels through the air to the ears of the people
inside the room.

You

can prove that sound goes through solid things.
Rest your head on the end of your table.
Stretch your arm and scratch the other end
of the table with your fingernails. You hear
the sound of the scratching through the table
top. You will be surprised how loud that little
scratch will sound.

The Indians knew

that rubbing causes heat and sometimes even starts a fire. They did not know about matches. They rubbed two dry pieces of wood together rapidly. Fine wood dust was made by the rubbing. At last the wood dust became so hot that it began to burn. With this burning wood dust the Indians started their fire.

Today

Boy Scouts sometimes use the Indian drill
to start a campfire.   The Boy Scouts
do know about matches but they do not
always use them when they are out camping.

You

can prove that rubbing causes heat.
Rub the palms of your hands together
quickly.   Do you feel the heat?

The Indians knew

how to make plants grow better. Since there
were more fish in the rivers, seas, and oceans
than the Indians could eat, they put some of
the fish they caught into the earth when they
planted corn or tomatoes. This made these
vegetables grow better.

Today

farmers feed the earth with animal waste and special plant foods to make their plants grow better.

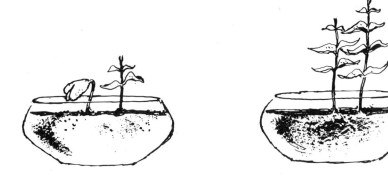

You

can prove to yourself that plant food makes plants grow better.

Soak a few dry lima beans overnight. The next morning, plant some of these beans in a dish of sand. Plant the rest of them in a dish of sand mixed with the special plant food which you can buy at any florist's. Water each dish daily for a week or so. Watch carefully to see which dish of beans grows better plants.

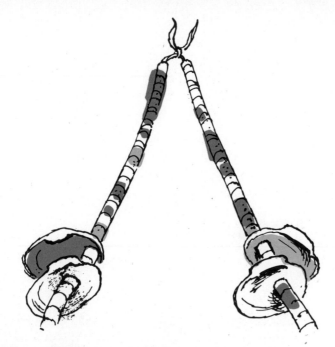

The Indians knew

that rubbing wears away things.
They made holes in clam shells and in oyster
shells by rubbing pointed stones against
them until a hole was worn into them.   They
used these shells to make strings of beads.

Today

the dentist drills teeth to rub away the
decayed parts of the teeth.
We drill for oil and we drill for well water.
The drilling wears away the rocks in the
earth.

You

can prove that rubbing makes things wear away.
Rub a nail file against your fingernails.
Watch the ends of your fingernails wear away.

The Indians knew

that many things float in water. They knew
that logs can float for long distances.
They cut down trees, tied several tree trunks
together to make a raft, and then went floating
down the river on these rafts.

Today

lumbermen go into the woods and cut down trees.
These logs are floated down the river to the
mill where they are cut up into boards.

You

can prove that some things float when they
are put into water.

Drop a nail, a piece of wood, a small stone,
and a coin into a basin of water. You will
see how each of these things will sink, except
the wood. This will float.

The Indians knew
how to use the moon as a calendar.
They knew that the full moon appears about
every twenty-nine days.

Today

the number of days in the month on our calendar is almost the same as the number of days in the "moon month" of the Indians.

You

too can use the moon as a calendar. Keep a record of the number of days it takes from one full face of the moon to the next full face of the moon.

Compare this with the number of days in the calendar month.

Now do you understand why we call this a moon month?

Now that you have read the book and you have done the activities, you have found out that the Indians did many things that we do today.

The Indians certainly knew how to use what they found around them.

Don't you think that we still make use of what we find around us?

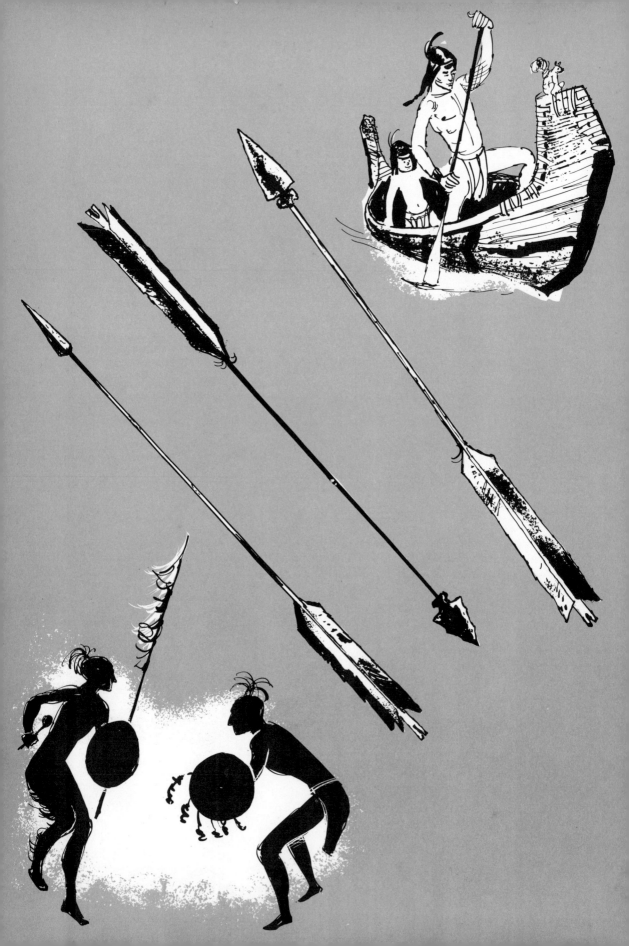